Coming home to her

Emily Juniper

Beyond all hope, I prayed those timeless

days we spent might be made twice as long.

•

I prayed one word: I want.

•

Someone, I tell you, will remember us

even in another time.

-*Sappho*

CONTENTS

Table of Contents iv

Dedication ix

Spring Cleaning 1

Drawn and quartered 2

Epiphany 3

Photosynthesis 4

Dig 5

Carnival 7

Soft 9

Hooked 10

Things I Buried 11

Unburied 12

Split 13

The soft, the safe… 14

New 15

Buzz 16

Someday 17

Bend Time 18

Le Sigh 20

Drowned 21

Weight 22

Kids these days 23

Essential Knots for Boys 24

Chemistry 25

If you tell her anything   26

Peel   27

THE DREAM   28

Untitled   29

Paradise Lost   30

Nihilism   31

Styrofoam cup   32

Not balloons   33

Don't   34

Reflection   35

Commitment issues   37

Maybe   39

Summer of 2020   40

Things we took for granted   41

Slaughter   42

Title   43

Flight risk   44

Smoking gun   45

The dance   46

My love language must be…   47

Used   48

218   49

Controlled burn   51

Sundrunk   52

Long Term Goals.   53

v

Promise   54

Twelve ribs   55

Milk & Honey   56

Two Faces   57

Red Thread of Fate   58

Forgive   59

Things I Lost Along the Way   60

Dude   61

Grey   62

Donnie Darko   63

Chernobyl   65

—   67

Apocalypse   68

Desire   69

Everywhere, everywhere   70

Covid thoughts   71

Chloe Rose   72

Silkworm   73

Rust   74

Do Androids Dream of Electric Sheep? 75

Evil eye   76

Spanish moss   77

Vulnerable   78

Duplicity   79

Thin lines   80

Cathedrals   81

The girl who played with fire   82

Hallelujah   83

Things that make me cry   85

Unravel   86

An argument for bovine pronouns   87

Unspoken   88

Tailor   89

Ogunquit   90

Breakfast Melancholy   91

Vor i Vaglaskogi   93

Golden Hour   95

Metamorphosis   96

Cicada   97

Kindle   98

For Ellie   99

Metronome   100

Satisfaction   101

The Awakening   102

And...   103

May Day   104

Notes   107

Afterward   108

About the Author   111

Excerpt from *Rafa and the Real Boy*   112

For my wife

Spring Cleaning

1. Open the windows and let in the light. Bask for a moment.

2. Shake out the rugs. Watch self-doubt and self-loathing flutter
   like butterfly wings to the ground below. From dust they came,
   to dust they shall return.

3. Dig out the old love letters from your underwear drawer. Burn them.
   They are only an illusion of warmth, and you deserve the real thing.

4. Scrub your skin raw and cut off your hair. Rid yourself of all the
   places she's touched. Show her your body is no longer a place she
   can come home to.

5. Take a deep breath, close your eyes for a beat, and welcome
   the Spring.

You have stretched me–
drawn,
quartered,
I have nothing left to give.

Drawn & quartered

I woke up one morning
and didn't recognize myself in the mirror.
Something was different,
though not altogether wrong.

It was the fire in my throat I'd never felt before
begging me to scream
and the ringing in my ears
demanding to be heard.

It was the longing in my chest that washed over me like
the siege of an ancient forest
by wildfire–

it was unforgiving,
but I didn't want it to stop.

Epiphany

They called us green and
perhaps we were.

For that summer,
we soaked up sunshine and rain
and seemed to grow
like only green things can.

Our roots intertwined like lifelines on hands
and our hands intertwined
like webs of light between stars in the night sky.

They called us green like it was a bad thing to
still believe in things no one else can see
(like damaged cells regenerating, like broken hearts
annulling all the cracks).

You'll understand when you're older
they'd tell us
but we didn't care that they were being condescending.
We just kept inhaling sweet sun
and exhaling as much goodness as we took in–
symbiosis.

If this life-giving process of you and I
isn't understanding,
then may God keep me ignorant forever.

Photosynthesis

Sometimes
I dig up things I know I shouldn't–
feelings, memories, other people's pasts.

I'm like a little girl
in a yellow Easter dress
who wants to dig up earthworms
before church.
I know I should leave them be,
but some things
crawl around just begging to be unearthed.

Dig

You were the essence of summer
with cut-off shorts and long, brown legs,
sticky-tongued with a wand of cotton candy in hand.

It was The World's Fair. Rochester, 2016.
We were ushered to a grungy seat
by that greasy carnie,
and you looked at me and laughed
when he winked at us but
neither of us minded
how tightly he strapped us in–
shoulder to shoulder,
skin to skin,
peaches and cream to toasted cinnamon-sugar.

He cranked a lever
and the floor beneath us sprang to life,
up, up, up,
a million miles into the air.
Up, up, up
where there were no drunk dads or
homophobic classmates
or any of the plagues that weighed us down.
Up there,
we were free to fly.

Our thighs brushed one another
like lazy hands hanging at sides as
we stole glances of the world
through ticking metal spokes,
the sunset flickering like a silent movie
(there and gone and back again).

I wished the movie'd never end,
but summer is fleeting
like carnivals

and first dates on ferris wheels
and two-token sweet escapes.

I guess you and I were, too.

Carnival

I am soft

like rain caressing windows
while the world sleeps,

thunder in the distance rumbles like a memory

and breath escaping lips in moments
of quiet understanding or longing or grace

and the things you reach for when you're hurting;
a craving without a name.

Come, let me be soft for you.
Let me show you something the world convinced you
you did not need and I promise,
you'll never want to go back
to a time when you did not know it.

Soft

Don't think about it, I tell myself, but if it doesn't work with the bad thoughts, why on earth would it work with you when you are so damn good. You're stuck in me, like electric signals coursing through my synapses or rich, red blood pumping through my veins–all feelings and oxygen and life. You're that rare nostalgia that doesn't hurt; a longing, a hunger, a dull, constant, wonderful ache. The hole filled with fire in the pit of my belly. *Don't think about it. Don't think about it.* I tell myself again and again, but here I am thinking about you anyway. And there you are, with your pretty face and your pretty hair and your beautiful mind.

There you are, just being you.

Hooked

Things I Buried

1. The first sex dream I ever had. I was fourteen, she was a year older. Olive skin, dark, wavy hair. Green eyes and spindly legs. I buried that so far down, it fertilized flowers on the other side of the globe.

2. My first dog. Dad pretended not to cry, and I pretended not to see. He dug the hole, and I painted the headstone. Tessie, 1999-2012. Her ashes still rest at 218 Warren Rd. amongst the wildflowers.

3. What J told us. We left it in the stale air of the car I no longer drive. I wonder if it sunk into the upholstery, and whether the new owners shiver when they feel the words ripple beneath their spines.

4. Feelings. So many feelings. Too much this, not enough that. I've hidden so many of them and now it's thirty years later and they are all coming back from the dead, skeleton fingers poking through the dry, un-watered ground. I thought if I ignored them, they would go away. But they are not hiccups, they are a mouthful of decaying teeth; three decades worth of cavities begging to be filled.

It was so close to being buried for good, deep down in the pit of my stomach. A parched plant pleading for water, wilting and begging to bloom. I hadn't nourished it in so long that it stopped asking to be fed. But that night, you dug it up. And it was surprising and beautiful and messy (digging up forgotten things always is) but not a bit confusing. And I just want you to know how grateful I am for whatever possessed you to pick up the shovel.

Unburied

I would split myself down the seams

if it meant that even half of me

could be with you.

Split

I wonder what the ground felt the first time it was touched by the rain?
Probably soft. And safe.
I wonder if the rain whispered *it's going to be okay*
as it filled up empty riverbeds with life.

The soft, the safe,
and the pounding—

like the blood that races through my veins
when your skin touches mine,
like two hearts beating beneath a river of white sheets.

The soft, the safe, the pounding, the *life.*

When I visit the Sahara before a great rain,
I'll know the anticipation of waiting,
and the relief of feeling alive once again.
When I visit the Sistine Chapel, I'll look up and know
what Adam felt when God sparked life into him with nothing but a touch.

The soft, the safe, the pounding, the *life.*

Look at us;
with our daffodil smiles,
the grown-up make believe,
and this insatiable good hurt that can barely be contained by
skin and bone.

It's like spotting heat lightning on the fourth of July
while everyone else drinks in cheap parking-lot fireworks.
It is new and unexpected and so undeniably welcome.
like surprise rain in the desert,
or a trickle of water
from a dried-up tap.

New

Buzz, buzz.

Like strong coffee
or honeybees to purple clover.

Like you, ricocheting around inside
my brain-

humming; melodic.

Zzz.

Buzz

Someday [suhm-day] adv.

A word often whispered in longing. The fornication
of melancholy and hope.

We seem to bend time,
you and I.

On late night calls,
seconds chase minutes
until whole hours are devoured by
the greedy belly of the night.

Then,
as soon as we crawl into bed
(alone)
the hours are vomited up.
Days regurgitate themselves over and over,
like cows chewing cud
in endless monotony
and we never get any closer to
feeling one another
in the flesh.

You asked
what I would want my superpower to be.
You asked if I'd travel through time and
my answer was
   no.

I don't want to go forward or back,
I want to pause our perfect moments.

Like the seconds before our lips touch for
the very first time
(because I know they will)
 or the time in the back of the uber
(the night you dug this up, the night I let it be unearthed).

My head on your shoulder,
your hair tickling my face,
the scent and feel of it as
constant and fluid as
I wish time could be
for us.

Bend Time...

                                        And now we're here,
                                        against all odds

                                 I, in the right place at the right time,
                                 You, the only home I'll ever need.

                        Candles lit, wine poured, and windows shut tight–

                                                -marry me-

                        I'd let you kiss my forehead in the back of an uber
                                                'til the end of time.

                                                ...Epilogue: 14. Nov. 20

Alone doesn't always mean
alone.

Sometimes alone just means
not with you.

Le Sigh

Like a sudden storm,
there was no warning when you let go.

Just a quick darkening of skies
and tears falling from the eyes of an angry, unforgiving God–
the one in the Old Testament
who drowned all the sinners without a trial.

Flooded gardens,
damp skin,
drowned cocoons still writhing in the mud
(butterfly dreams, no more)
and you, gone, like the sun before the rain.

Drowned

Sometimes we pray for the weight to be lifted.

Sometimes, we don't even know it exists
and when it is finally lifted,
we are so light
we fly.

Weight

I need new sneakers
but I pretend these fit just fine
because mom works two jobs
and dad would rather buy beer than tennis shoes.

I need to do my homework
but my sister needs to eat
so macaroni has to come before fractions
(1/2 cup milk, 1/3 cup butter).

I need sleep
but my mind won't shut up
and my teachers gonna say I'm lazy 'cause I
can't stay awake in class.

I need hope
but there isn't any light
and I'm starting to think the tunnel is a hole
that goes down, down, down,
no light, no end.

I need a bag
but they don't make 'em big enough to
hold all the things I carry
and I need someone to listen but
I never learned to speak.

Kids these days

My brother had a book
called *Essential Knots for Boys*
and just to spite the title
I studied it until
I could tie boats to docks
and old tires to trees
and ropes to limbs over watering holes.

All these knots but
what a shame,
I never learned to untie them
and though it's no big deal
that the tire swing still hangs in the backyard,

I fear the knot in my throat may never,
ever come undone.

Essential Knots for Boys

You,
all warm flesh
and raw soul
and pumping blood;
a beautiful mess like me.

I,
a fool to think
we could ignore this
when carbon has a half-life of
six-thousand years and we are
nothing
if not organic.

It's radioactive, my dear.
It won't just trickle away.

Chemistry

If you tell her anything,
tell her I am not a ghost,
that I do not linger in the crevices of your attic
(or the folds of your brain)
like spirits of lost-love often do.

Tell her that I was a house,
but she is a home you never want to leave and
always yearn to return to.
That all of the holes
I bore in you have been filled and
re-drilled to fit only her key.

Tell her I was Andromeda,
swirling in your summer sky
but she is the whole damn Cosmos
and that you want to drift, weightless
into her abyss.

Tell her whatever it takes
to quiet the uncertainty in her mind
but most importantly of all,

never
ever
tell her
you are lying.

If you tell her anything

Of course it's going to take a while to
feel okay.

Like peeling off a sunburn
to reveal pink skin underneath,

sometimes we must shed a layer
before the new can grow.

Peel

THE DREAM

I walk into the bathroom, and look in the mirror. Not only do I recognize the person staring back, but I know who she is and I like her. Sometimes, even love her. I smile and she smiles back, and her jaw isn't clenched like she might be biting through her cheek behind a guise of manufactured joy. There are blemishes on her face but they are the color of peonies or poppies, not walking-through-the- hallway-head-bowed-hoping-no-one-sees. Her lips are petal smooth, not cracked and bleeding from picking. I look at her again, her smile recedes like a peaceful wave from the shore, knowing it can always come back. Now she doesn't force it. Now she's comfortable. Satisfied. Content. She's accepted herself just the way she is. She looks away, I look away. Head full of clementines and first-snow feels and songs, not emptiness. And I think, *this is how it feels to finally wake up. This is how it feels to have bloomed.*

Lakeside
rain pokes at the water
like little fingers into vanilla cake batter.

I feel the thunder in my bones
signaling a new season
not summer, not autumn,
a new season of me.

Lightning strikes
like cliches out of my mouth
and I wonder
if you'll remember me
and if you do
I hope it doesn't hurt.

Untitled

There you are,
ultraviolet on a backdrop of black and white,
technicolor dreams shattering the glass ceiling of lonely film noir nights.

And there they are,
straight lines
not meant to be crossed,
no matter how desperately we may want to.

And here I am, caught
between right and
~~wrong~~ right.

I'll tell you what it's like;

it's like reading *Paradise Lost*
and not knowing whether to root
for the devil or God.

Paradise Lost

I wake up early
and make my breakfast
(we call it *bacon* not *pig flesh*
because it's easier to digest that way).

Later
I hand money to a cashier
at Zara
to pay for a new blouse and
for a child to remain indentured
in a country I don't even know exists.

It's funny
because I often look at the stars
and think no one will remember me once I'm gone,

but today
I purchased death and slavery
and I don't think anyone forgets
the one who kills them
or the one who keeps them in chains.

Nihilism

On my way to work
I see a man with
leathered skin,
hollow eyes
and a styrofoam cup
held out to passersby who pass on by.

I thought styrofoam was banned in this city but
we're still okay
with homelessness.

Without thinking, I hold out a dollar but
I'm not sure if it's altruism or guilt,
or if there's even a difference between the two
anymore.

Styrofoam cup

I can still hear the weeping willows
behind our home
whispering
come back, come back.

Their branches drift sadly, carelessly
like snapped strings on violins
or red balloons held by children who do not understand
that once you release something,
you cannot coax it back with words.

Not backyards,
not people.

Not youth,
and not balloons.

Not balloons

Don't tell me I am everything,

that you love me just the way I am
(always have, always will)

that I am living proof
there is a God and then leave.

Don't give me pretty words
just to take them all away.

Don't

Maybe I don't know you as well as I thought
I say.

Maybe you never really tried,
the mirror says back.

Reflection

I grab the shovel
and start the car
slowly,
quietly
as if it matters.
As if you'd need to hear the sound of the ignition to
know I'm running away.

When you wake up missing something,
you'll know.
You'll inhale sharply
and feel a hole,
because the contents of your chest cavity
will be beating faintly in the passenger seat beside me as
I drive away from the home we built together.

The night guard
opens the gates to the cemetery
without even asking my business.
It's like going to your favorite diner
and not having to order;
he already knows what I'm here for,
and it ain't pancakes.

Again?
He asks
as I nod and turn away
because he's judging me.
It's okay;
I'm judging me too.

I find an empty plot near the back,
fall to my knees,
and say a prayer my grandmother taught me.

Holy Mary, mother of God, pray for us sinners now
and at the hour of our deaths

I weep a little
then lay our love to rest next
to all the others
I was too afraid to try to keep.

Commitment issues

Maybe it's over
or maybe
it never began.

Maybe
I was a shy rainstorm
they predicted on the evening news
that didn't come to fruition

or maybe
I was the white noise
that lulled you to sleep,

never tangible enough
to be heard over the commotion
of all your other dreams.

Maybe

This isn't a poem,
I don't know how to write poetry anymore. I've been stuck in my house since March with nothing but toilet paper, bottled water, and news.

News.

They broke into Breonna Taylor's home in the middle of the night because they thought there *might* be drugs there, and now she's **dead.**

Did you know we're in the middle of the 6th mass extinction?
But what is fauna compared to
the **filthy bed** the oil companies and politicians share.

Why does the color of my state
determine my quality of healthcare if I'm **trans**?
(I'm not, but that's not the point).

How do I write platitudes
when five black men were found hanging from trees
and all of them were *suicides.*

How do I write about **love**
in a world so full of **hate.**

Summer 2020

A best friend's laugh/ my mother's arms/ that little bar on Lark with my girlfriend on a Friday night/ weekends away from home/ anything away from home/ school/ school/ *school*/ The Wailin' Jennys in Boston/ grandparents, graduations, and prom/ walking past a neighbor without feeling afraid/ a trip to the store without paranoia/ sunshine without darkness/ a life without a lock.

Things we took for granted

I used to say
I don't know how slaughterhouse workers live with themselves
because I could never take a paycheck
in exchange for a gentle life that wasn't even mine to barter with.

But then I realized
I was the one putting money in the slaughter-man's hand.

So who's the bad guy:
the one with the knife on the killing room floor,
or the one in a clean, white room
paying for it to be done behind closed doors?

Slaughter

Your lips touch mine and I taste the sun—
fire,
honey,
celestial magic.

They'll call me the woman
who burned alive
and lived.

When you asked me to slow down
I thought you meant to chew my food a little more
or drive in the right lane
or stop drinking wine like it's a tall glass of water.

When you asked me to slow down, I
thought you meant
Let's take our time
and see where this can go
not
I'm getting ready to run.

Flight risk

I walk alone at night
through fields of fireflies
and lilac drifts down my throat
like smoke from the cigarettes you used to hold between two fingers

inhale, exhale.

I wonder about you-
who you're with,
where you are in the summertime,
whether or not you wonder
about me too.

I wonder if those two fingers point to me
like a compass
or a smoking gun.

Smoking gun

Our bodies find each other
like honeybees;
body chemicals and
soft vibrations in the air from miles away.

I am your queen
now, come
and get your honey.

The Dance

MY LOVE LANGUAGE MUST BE...

Sprigs of eucalyptus in the shower and honey in my tea. Breakfast (or not) in bed on a lazy Saturday. Toothpaste kisses. Making music with our hands, painting numbers down your spine. Your thumb on my tear-stained cheek. Not having to hide my obsessions or compulsions, not having to explain why I don't use a knife. Novocain and red wine. The part in the story where people become homes.

Used -
cars
tissues
textbooks
me, at sixteen and twenty-two.

You didn't mean it
but the things you do not mean still
hurt
for I am not mechanical or
cotton
or paper;
I am feelings and friction and flesh.

Used

I watch my mother crosshatch honey over yogurt,
morning sun

    d
     r
      i
       p
        s

through a window time has frozen shut.
This old house has stories
no one else will ever know–

Talking smack and pulling weeds,
walks through the creek
(just take your tevas off and let your feet feel the river stones,
these spiders don't bite)
the secret door
in the second daughter's bedroom
(I'd sneak to use the internet, she'd sneak to kiss her boyfriend)
paint splatter tattooed on my bedroom wall.

Christmas mornings, house full of cinnamon,
black bear in the backyard,
half-drowned dog pulled from the river
(she lived thirteen years after that)

I left one year
and came back in October
loving my mother more than I ever had before
because it's true
that distance makes the heart grow fonder.

Each year someone else left

until six became
five
became
four
became
three
became two

and then two moved to the lake
and now all that's left are the ashes on the hill,
the cat buried in the garden,
a for-sale sign,
and sixteen years of memories swallowed by the wood
my father stained with his own hands.

2 1 8

Ashes
are all that's left of us
as you slink back to where you came from,
saying *a good burn is healthy for a forest.*

But let me tell you;
what's good for the forest
isn't always
good for the tree.

Controlled burn

Heavy eyes,
heart beating in the heat

Pulse in your neck,
racing

A brush of air,
salty

The sand, rough
our skin, soft
the water, endless
the day, swollen

You,
sundrunk,
coming
only
only
only

for me.

Sundrunk

Long Term Goals

1. Drink more water. Sometimes, I get so dehydrated my cells begin to shrivel. *Apoptosis* is fun to say, but much more of it and I'll be half a human.

2. Buy less, travel more. Live in abundance with people and places, not things.

3. Stop picking flowers and feet. Let the flowers live, let my calluses heal. I don't need a daisy's petals to know you love me any more than I need anxiety scabs under foot when I walk.

4. Erase the word "calorie" from my vocabulary. No, murder it. Burn it, bury it, walk away, and never look back.

5. Learn how to conduct electricity through my body, from one fingertip to the other. Out of you, into me, without combusting spontaneously. I'm weary of catching fire, but I cannot resist the heat.

She said
I promise you, it will always be okay to be human
and I never realized how badly
I needed those words until I heard them.

They nestled up inside the coils of my ear like
sleeping butterflies and whispered
that it was safe for me to build a home within myself,
and so I did.

And so must you.

Promise

It is said that on the sixth day,
God took a rib from Adam,
planted it in the earth and grew Eve
so that he would feel less alone.

I press my fingers into my side
and palpate the grooves that run down my body
like ridges cut into a mountainside,
half expecting to count only eleven
> *because it has only ever been a woman*
> *who could make me feel whole*
but counting twelve,
> *because I didn't have to sacrifice*
> *a part of myself to prove it to her.*

Twelve ribs

(S)he has skin like warm honey
but I am alabaster
like a marble countertop.

Drip, drip
(s)he spills onto me
and there's something to be said
for being unclean.

Milk & Honey

I look in the mirror and see two faces:

The woman I am with you,
and the woman I am with me.

You split me down the seams
like I was sewn together with rotted thread
and you did it so slowly,
I didn't even feel you tear me
from myself.

Two faces

You and I floated through space
(the moon, the sun, and all of Saturn's rings)
and got caught–
two flecks of stardust in the eyes of a god
who picked us out and unfolded us like a passed note in class,
who watched squid-black ink spill from the belly of the universe
like petrol onto the skeleton of time.

I used to think we couldn't have it all

but

fate dips her quill in the ink
and writes us into a sentence,
a storybook,
a whole beautiful life

while

we dip our red thread in the spilled gasoline,
light a match and let it burn–
a hungry fire that can't be put out.

Red thread of fate

Plant a seed,
look to the east,
and wait.

Notice your back no longer hurting
and your jaw no longer clenching
and a single green tip poking through the dirt–
proof that beauty can grow on the grave of a grudge.

Resentment is crippling;
a cage only forgiveness can free you from.

Forgive

Things I Lost Along the Way

1. Half of every pair of socks I've ever owned.

2. A grandfather, a big house, two dogs, and a cat. Four people I will always, always love. My best friend.

3. My sanity; once or twice. My way, more times than I can count.

4. The self-loathing that used to follow me like a hungry dog. I buried it in the ground and flowers grow there in spite of it all.

Dude makes me feel special by comparing me to other women he's been with. Dude cheats on me with other women. Dude probably tells them the same thing he told me. Dude's words mean nothing now, even the ones that felt so real. Dude comes out of the woodwork every now and then to keep me on a string. I'm a kitten and he's dangling a ball of yarn. Dude wishes me a Happy Birthday and says "I hope you're doing well..." once a year, even half a decade later. Dude doesn't know my walls are made of glass and I can see him coming from ten miles away. Dude doesn't know the walls are unbreakable. Dude tells me how pretty I am and tries to touch me through the glass. I smile.

I tell Dude to keep on walking.

Dude

All of my favorite things
are in-betweens,

like dawn and dusk,
or the moments before our lips touched for
the first time
      (a fold in time no one else will ever feel).

Like almost breaking the rules–but not quite
and rainbows between the sun and storm.

Like the suspense of waiting for something that makes your heart leap,
watching a cut transform from fissure to scar and witnessing the strength
of the human ability to heal.

Like the moment between the jump and the splash
      (skinny dipping in the lake at night)
or the instant your head hits my pillow after a long day,
just before drifting off to sleep.

Grey gets a bad rap,
but I think it's the color of almost everything.

Grey

I feel him following me
like a memory,
a shadow,
Frank
from that movie about the
schizophrenic kid
(demonic rabbits and the end of the world)
I wonder, Donnie,
am I mad too?

I find it kind of funny, I find it kind of sad, the
dreams in which I'm dying are the best I've ever had

Or will I wake up
Twenty-eight days ~~later~~ ago
like none of this
ever happened?

Donnie Darko

Chernobyl
I sing the word,
you shiver and go pale
and something, somewhere burns
(still)
after all these years.

Chernobyl
Like a dormant virus,
a collective memory awakens
of a faraway place on a map
where all the pointed fingers used to meet
to play world-wide blame games.

чорнобиль
We learned to pronounce this foreign word
because when you're afraid of something,
you learn its fucking name.

Chernobyl
we see radiation burns
and red flags with yellow sickles cutting through contaminated air
like acid rain cutting through lead paint
on old Soviet statues.

Chernobyl
they said 31 died
only 31
but what about the fallout?
The helicopters, snapped like dollar store bobby bins
and stillborns with too many limbs?
And what sarcophagus could hide 93,000 thyroid tumors?

Calloway
Atucha

Ginna

Hanul
Almaraz
Oconee

Embalse
Kozloduy,
Point Lepreau

Suddenly,
you are not quite sure what this poem is about
because these are names you do not know.

Tell me,
why do we learn the names of the ones who've hurt us
but not the ones of those
with all the power to do the same?

Chernobyl

Purple flames torch the sky like napalm
as eight billion voices scream in unison
then fall silent,
corpses glowing
beneath a mushroom the size of the sun.

I am become death, the destroyer of worlds.

Only cockroaches will survive these violent delights,
but this is what we asked for,

right?

It was a Saturday in November, the day the planes fell out of the sky. We promised we'd find each other at the end of t h e world so I waited at our sacred spot, the one down by the river where the wild ferns grow.

The smoke and the ash came,
but you never did.

Apocalypse

Desire

1. The crescendo of my favorite song; the anticipation as good as the climax itself.

2. Autumn. Fall air, candle in the window, pumpkin cookies in the oven. Soccer cleats and grass clippings on the white tile floor. The scent of my mother's dark brown hair when she gathers me into her arms after a long season apart.

3. Tiptoes. Eight years old. Reaching with a soup spoon for the sugar hidden in the back of the forbidden cupboard. Little crystals dissolving on my tongue.

4. The wet sand when waves recede. The shore, missing its blanket. *Ebb, flow. Desire, fulfillment.* The beautiful white noise of an eternal dance.

5. You, my favorite song. *(see #1)*

It was like dipping cupped hands
into the ocean–

so much of you everywhere,
but nothing I could quite hold onto.

Everywhere, Everywhere

I go to the river alone
to feel the green of spring

I want to be a dryad when I grow up.

I crouch,
pretending to make leaves bloom
when I can hardly keep the bookshelf-aloe alive.

But this poem isn't about death
no, there's been enough of that this year.
This poem is about
dryads and daisies
and green and gratitude
and rivers and rain

for though my poor thumb was never very green
I've gotten good
at keeping love and hope alive
even through seasons of intense, blackening dark.

COVID thoughts

She smells of a spring night,
breeze brushing tattooed shoulders
just warm enough not to need a coat.

Crickets and fireflies,
daffodils poking through the garden floor
with yellow fingers.

Clear sky, bright moon,
someone vaping down Congress Street
lined with cherry blossoms, half asleep.

An absinthe cocktail,
black licorice on my tongue,
a couple that looks like us.

Rose petals in the bath,
leaves unfurling on trees
that've stood guard
since before we were born.

She smells of a spring night
and a pinky promise
I never will forget.

Chloe Rose

Your voice slides
like silk sheets
over me
into me
little vibratos
of soft grey wings

work, work, work,
tiny silver worms,
Thailand's honey,
crunching mouths spin a red thread
no shears dare cut.

Tie it to me,
Tie it to you,
Some couples weave a tightening noose
while others embroider
pretty crimson stitches
in the fabric of eternity.

Silkworm

Like copper, we rusted
because tears and rain can't heal everything

and some things are meant to disintegrate.

R u s t

I saw her through honey colored glasses—
where dusk was golden even on a cloudy night
and when I touched her, my fingers turned to amber,
caramel, sweet, and ready to fossilize.

They say the greatest love stories have already been written
yet here we are, two hearts beating,
fluttering wings,
moths to flames that electrify
but do not aim to kill.

We may never know if androids dream of electric sheep,
but I can say with absolute certainty
I only dream of you.

Do Androids Dream of Electric Sheep?

They tell me my necklace is backwards,
the pendant, turned the wrong way.

It's an evil eye and the only thing I seem to need protecting from these days
lies under my own skin.

I tell them this and they back away,
but I am not a threat to anyone.

I just haven't figured out how to protect me from myself.

Evil Eye

I hang to the words that drip from your lips
(and ooze from your fingers to my phone)
like Spanish moss to old southern trees
and I worry that maybe I am
clingy or needy
or too damn hopeful.

But the Spanish moss needs a home
and the tree grows lonely in eternity;
all that life and no one to share it with.

What are the trees without their drapery, anyway
but naked and alone?
And what good is the moss, weeping on the ground?

It makes me wonder if needing someone
has to be such a bad thing,
after all.

Spanish Moss

Sometimes
I am so
in my feelings
I begin to turn inside out.

My insides
are where my outsides should be
and I am exposed
like a shaved head in the winter or
a pillow without its case.

Now (I think) you see all of me,
every thought I haven't finished thinking,
and every word before my tongue even knows where
to click my teeth to bring it to life.

Every secret, every heartache, every hope, and every hurt.

At first it was frightening
to think you knew the real me,
but then you did
and liked me all the same.

Is this what it means to be vulnerable with someone?
To feel naked,
but for once not so ▮▮▮▮ alone?

Vulnerable

Pure
like bread bleached white with chemicals;
always a facade.

Hooked
a fishing lure through a translucent lip.

Chemistry
homemade napalm and blistering virgin lungs.

...See how readily the properties of love can turn destructive?

Duplicity

I do not know if I am a good person who did a bad thing,
or a bad person,
the antagonist of my own story, or yours
and I don't know if I will ever know for sure.

You see,
the grey line is tightrope-thin
and the referee in my head isn't
any good at making calls
and all the spectators want to do is criticize a game
they have no idea how to play.

Thin Lines

You built me a cathedral
before I learned to pray.

How did you know what I needed,
before I even knew

myself?

Cathedrals

I struck a match,
set my skirt ablaze,
then ran around the village
crying out for water and
pulling fire alarms
as if someone had done it to me.

As if I were not the one
who burned my own castle to the ground just to
see what the skyline would look like painted
blistering orange.

The ~~boy~~ girl who ~~cried~~ lit ~~wolf~~ herself on fire

There aren't enough prayers in my language to
thank the Lord for delivering you to me.
If I fell to my knees with clasped hands and milky eyes
and pled gratitude for the rest of my unholy life
it still wouldn't be enough.

I used to break to pieces in the kitchen like a wedding plate.
You'd pick me up, tie me to a broken chair
and keep me breathing even when I wanted it to end.
You would press two fingers to my neck and
feel a pulse that beat in time like song
(*the fourth, the fifth, the minor fall, the major lift*)
and remind me that red rivers flow through me
for a reason,
even if I do not understand.

And somehow
through all of the begging and breaking
you still loved me;
a pauper with a tongue that only knew how to form your name
and *I'm sorry, I'm sorry, I'm so sorry*
and the cold and broken syllables of a song
to which we knew the melody but not the meaning.

Hallelujah
the marble arch,
the victory march,
the Lord of song,
and the God who doesn't care for music.

Who only accepts payment for life-debt in breath,
each rise and fall of my chest
ticking me one step closer to a grave
I no longer lay in just see how it would feel
to try on death.

For the record,
I'll draw every breath I have for you
even when I want to stop
because at least then,
I'll know I'm living for something.

And Hallelujah,
the light beyond the veil is no longer something I chase because
I've got all the light I need
right here
in me.

Hallelujah

Things That Make Me Cry

1. Kids and teachers too afraid to go to school, wounds I caused but cannot fix, foie gras, veal farms, war.

2. A happy ending, a painful one, or no proper ending at all. *Ambiguous loss.*

3. Abandoned homes, empty nests, and for-sale signs. Sad windows, attics full of memories, and no one to share them with.

4. Singing children. Mountain summits. Missed connections. Arms worthy of being run into. The collective human experience of finally (finally) finding a place to belong.

5. San Junipero, Terabithia, and all of our secret places. *Here*, there, and anywhere we are.

You and I unraveled like yarn.

Once tightly balled, we hang on
by turquoise threads

and pretend it's fate so we don't have
to admit we're glorifying
a tangled mess.

Unravel

It is just a cow. But *it* has globes for eyes that soak me up like melted butter into soft, warm bread. And *its* breath on my hand is so prickling with life, how can *it* be a thing and not a soul? And *it* walks and jumps and nuzzles *its* kin and cries when *it* is afraid, just like I do, and just like you do, too. *It* hides from the thunder and the dark and doesn't like to be alone. And when *it* smells red iron rivers and sees the steel glint of the knife, *it* cries out for comfort, even if *it* doesn't quite know why. And aren't *we* all worthy of comfort? I think so, but *she* cannot be part of *we* if you only ever let yourself think of her as an *it.*

AN ARGUMENT FOR BOVINE PRONOUNS

A toddler throws a tantrum in aisle seven
and a jar of olives shatters on the floor.

I understand her, I think.
How difficult it is to know what you want,
but not be able to say so.

Like how I wanted you to
stay but couldn't find the words
to ask you not to leave.

Unspoken

I am a tailor.
I take broken things
-hearts-pride-ego-bones-
and stitch them back together with words
as if letters can be spun into thread.
My pen, the thimble between you and the blade,
the pointed tip of my tongue.
(thumb, needle, prick, *ouch*)

I think sometimes if I could sew a quilt out of sorrows
maybe,
just maybe
I could find a way to keep you warm
through all the pain
even if I was the one
who was careless with the
scissors and cut you in the first
place.

Tailor

The moon
the tide
Push, pull
in, out
ebb, flow

Swollen water
in and out
the curtains,
the sheets,
the pulse of the night

Push, pull
in and out
the moon, the tide,
your breath and mine

The waves
the night
You, me
ebb, flow,
repeat.

Ogunquit

You like eggs in the morning.

Over easy or scrambled,
with orange juice, freshly squeezed.
I'd always ask if you wanted toast,
knowing you'd say no
because of carbs or calories
though I don't think any amount of bread
could make you less attractive if it tried.

It's funny how intimate it is,
getting to know someone's routine.
Knowing how they take their coffee
             coconut milk, no sugar
knowing if they brush their teeth before or after
             you're a before, I'm an after
knowing where they keep their toothbrush
             letting me keep mine there, too.

I sometimes wonder whose toothbrush
lives in the pink cup under your sink
now.

Breakfast Melancholy

VOR I VAGLASKOGI

(f o r   y o u)

Look at us. We are so busy pointing fingers and building walls and dropping bombs that we forget how much we have in common.

We forget that when we look up at the night sky, we see the light of the same moon no matter what god we pray to. We forget that the word for mother sounds the same in almost any language, and that we were all born from one. We forget that when we shake hands with the refugee family at church, their skin will feel the same as ours, only thicker.

We forget that we don't need to understand the lyrics to feel the meaning of a song. *Vor i Vaglaskogi* sends shivers down my spine, though I don't know a word of Icelandic. (This is what you meant, I think, when you spoke of making emotion out of sound.) We forget that there are languages only recorded in memory and touch that connect us like strings of a spider's web; flexible, sticky, and strong.

Let me ask you this; have you ever looked at someone you love and wondered why you can't find the words to tell them how you feel? Of course you have. Have you ever felt someone else's skin beneath your fingers and wondered how you ever lived without the color of their touch? Have you ever cried to a stranger and not been able to thank them for letting you, because they got off the train before you had the chance? Of course you have, of course you have.

The greatest lie I have ever been told is that we need to know someone's language to understand them. The truth is, love is a language all its own. So is gratitude. So is feeling heaven in the night sky, and hearing a beautiful song in a tongue I'll never comprehend. *Leikur í ljósum lokkum hinn vaggandi blær, the wind is counting your hair.*

How different the world would be if we focused a little more on the things we can all understand, and a little less on what language we tell our stories in.

Thighs,
golden from the sun
like saffron
or the hour
or my baby summer hair.
Golden like the lattes
from the cafe down the street.

It's easy with us,
sitting under a canopy of trees,
the light from above filtering through,
talking books and music and poetry and whether or not God exists
as if we could possibly know.
We read Sophocles and Shakespeare and Sappho-

> *Beyond all hope, I pray those timeless days we spent*
> *may be made twice as long.*

I know it sounds like we're full of ourselves
but really, we're just full of each other
and sunshine
and summer
and honey
and heat.

Golden thighs
golden eyes
and turmeric lattes.

Golden Hour

As children we are taught
that a caterpillar *becomes* a butterfly—

Eat, sleep, wake up beautiful.

But the truth is a caterpillar dissolves from the inside out
and must split itself down the seams
like sausage casing or too-tight pants
if it ever hopes to fly.

The body turns to sludge
around a heart and brain that stay in-tact—
a reminder that the universe likes us to pay for beauty with pain.

> *We all want to come back from the dead,*
> *but don't want to remember how it feels to die.*

This year my skin split open like the sky after a storm
and I had to fight like hell through chaos to reach grace.

I let myself dissolve
and emerged a changeling,
finally spreading wings I never knew I had
(I hid more than butterfly wings from myself
for twenty-nine years).

And though I'm grateful,
I will never take for granted the cost
of *becoming*
in a world that wanted me to stay exactly as I was.

Metamorphosis

We are shells of what we used to be;

dead cicadas on the sidewalk,

no more music, no more buzz.

Cicada

You. Me. That first night.

It was like throwing a match
onto an ocean of propane.

Kindle

Somewhere a man is crawling into bed with a woman he's trying to love but can't because your magnetism is pulling him away like a thirsty hound to water. He can't explain how he knows but he knows.

And somewhere a woman is sitting in a studio apartment in New York that she struggles to afford, sketching an ivory dress lined with lace. She's nobody now, but in three years her dress will hang in the window of the exact shop you'll walk by with your mother and you will know right away that it's the one. You won't know how you'll know, but you will.

And somewhere a house is being built by a woman and her wife who will move out in four years' time after their twins arrive, and the little bungalow will be empty at just the right time in just the right place at just the right price.

And though you sleep alone tonight and wonder why things never go your way, just know that your person is coming, the white dress you'll wear when you marry them is being imagined, and the house you'll share until you are old and grey is being built. The universe works in strange and mysterious ways and a life cannot be grown overnight like magic beans.

It is curating something just for you. Believe that.

For Ellie

I hear waves in the distance
and see water, the color of eyes.
The air is thick with salt
like the taste of your neck in the summertime.

We collect shells and coral and memories,
pretty skeletons of things long past
but we are here–
steady, present,
as alive as the endless metronome
of waves crashing in the night.

Metronome

Satisfaction. [sat-is-fak-shuhn] n.

The feeling of fulfillment; gratification.

A sharp razor singing against taught skin; the sound of a butter knife scraping across warm toast. Standing under a waterfall, completely clothed. Sweat-drenched skin after a hard run on a summer day. Teeth cutting through the first bite of a crisp Macintosh apple, just plucked from its tree. The whole month of October. The pop of a plugged ear (euphoria). The peeling skin of last week's sunburn. Listening to rain fall into a puddle; *drip drop, drip drop.*

Your hands on me, my hands on you; finally.

My fingers trace spines of books
and they purr open,
unleashing thoughts and words and memories
no one will ever understand in the same way I do.

I'll tell you a secret–
some Sunday mornings,
I pretend to write poetry about books
while I think about my hand on the small of your back
(painting vertebrae like numbers)
and wonder what it would be like to
open you up in the same way.

The Awakening

You are always bracing yourself
for the "but,"
for the guillotine drop
and the strings
attached and the hurt.

-But-

what if this time,
there are only good things to say?
No rolling
heads and no
despair.

What if this time, we are all *ands*-
only adding, never taking away:
You plus Me,
not *I love you,*
but.

What if this time it's a house in the woods and the sound of birds and bees
at coffee time. And trips to New Zealand and Istanbul and Patagonia and
down the street to the grocery store, hand in hand. And kissing and holding
and reading and falling asleep entangled. And knowing you'll never have to
be alone again, even when it is cold and dark and hard to bear. And ending
the same way we began, arms wrapped around one another, sharing the
same inch of breath.

And, and, and-

And everything you can possibly imagine.

A N D...

And

after all this time-
the endless lonely nights
the rejection that stung like bees
the sour taste of near-defeat-

you are rising like the sun herself,
a shining tribute to all the flowers we thought were lost under
the heavy blanket of winter,
then surprised us by clawing through the earth on
the first of May.

Remember that you are the red tulip on May Day, and
you shall never be uprooted.

May Day

And soon enough, coming home to her
just felt like *coming home*.

Juniper

Notes:

Page 26: *If You Tell Her Anything* was a writing prompt created by @madison_wells.

Page 47: *My Love Language Must Be…*was a writing prompt created by @zanefrederickswrites.

Page 61: *Dude* was inspired by a writing prompt created by @amykaypoetry.

Page 63: This poem is a reference to the 2001 film *Donnie Darko.*

Page 67: *I am become death, the destroyer of worlds* is from Hindu scripture, and was famously quoted by Robert Oppenheimer upon the detonation of the first atomic bomb.

Page 75: *Do Androids Dream of Electric Sheep?* Is a Sci-Fi novel by Philip K Dick.

Page 83: This poem is in reference to *Hallelujah,* a song written and recorded by Leonard Cohen.

Page 93: *Vor i Vaglaskogi* is a song by Kaleo.

Page 95: In *Golden Hour, 'Beyond all hope, I pray those timeless days we spent may be made twice as long'* is a quote from the Greek poet, Sappho.

Page 102: The title of this piece is in reference to the novel *The Awakening,* by Kate Chopin.

"In short, she was beginning to realize her position
in the universe as a human being, and to recognize her relations as an
individual to the world within and about her…but the beginning of things,
of a world especially, is necessarily vague, chaotic, and exceedingly
disturbing. How few of us ever emerge from such a beginning."

-Kate Chopin, *The Awakening*

ABOUT THE AUTHOR

Emily Juniper is the author of three other poetry collections (*Things I Learned in the Night, A Strangely Wrapped Gift,* and *Swim*) and one YA novel (*Rafa and the Real Boy*) as well as a few guided journals for mindfulness. She writes about love and loss, sexuality and coming out, femininity, and the trials and tribulations of growing up. She currently resides in upstate New York and is an advocate for mental health in teens and young adults. In her spare time, she enjoys writing, volunteering at farm animal sanctuaries, iced coffee, snuggling with her pup, and working with young writers.

You can find Emily on Instagram & TikTok
@by.emilyjuniper

EXCERPT FROM "RAFA AND THE REAL BOY," BY EMILY JUNIPER

SOME LOVES LAST A LIFETIME. SOME, LONGER...

Rafa
and the
Real Boy

Emily Juniper

CHAPTER 21

I open my eyes and for the first time in weeks, my senses are crystal clear. No heaviness in my head, no ringing in my ears, no lights floating near the ceiling. I am conscious of each breath as it passes through my nose, into my lungs, and travels out again. The sky is so bright that I can make out everything around me even though it must be nearing midnight. The moonlight is trickling through my window like a waterfall, full and incandescent. I see a mug of green tea on my nightstand that I vaguely remember Mom bringing up earlier as I hovered between sleep and consciousness. It's cold now, undrinkable.

I plant both of my feet firmly on the ground and it's surprisingly warm. Usually the old wood floors are cold and clammy at this hour, but not tonight. In fact, my whole body feels pleasantly warm, as if I just stepped out of a sauna. I slip on my moccasins, walk over to the bay window, and sit down on the padded window seat. I look at the brilliant moon against the star-dotted sky, which is indigo blue and endless. I hover in a trance – for how long, I cannot say– and only snap out of it when I hear someone calling out to me.

"Rafa!"

I look down. It's unbelievable, but it's…Ash. He's in my yard wearing only a t-shirt, though it can't be more than thirty-five or forty degrees. I check the time on my phone, and it's exactly midnight. I watch the time turn to twelve-oh-one and the date rolls from October 31 to November 1. I realize I completely missed handing out candy to trick-or-treaters, but that's okay. It's not like many of them would've made it to the creepy stone house at the end of the street.

"What are you doing?" I whisper, the air so clear that the sound of my voice carries for miles. He motions for me to join him on the lawn, and despite the strange nature of this situation there's no question in my mind that I'm going to accept his invitation. I slip my silky grey robe on overtop my white cotton sleep shorts and camisole, and briefly consider putting on a pair of sweatpants before deciding against it–I have nice legs.

I tiptoe down the stairs and through the kitchen where Benny is dreaming of squirrels. His back legs are twitching, and his muzzle is pulled over his teeth in a snarl. It isn't difficult to creep by without waking him.

"You make a terrible watchdog, Benny.

I ease open the latched glass door, not risking the front door as it's heavy and it creaks. I carefully shut it behind me and slink out into the night.

Ash is waiting for me in the yard. He holds out his arms and when I close the space between us, he embraces me. I run into him without thinking, it's almost instinctual. Even against the crisp November air, his hug is warm and comforting, like a mug of hot chocolate on a cold winter night, and though I'm not wearing a jacket, there isn't a single goosebump on my silver skin.

I still don't know what we are, if anything, but it doesn't seem to matter. All the hours I spent wondering why he keeps disappearing, or whether or not he actually cares seem silly and fruitless now. Of course he cares. He doesn't need to say it for me to know. We let go of one another after an embrace that lasts longer than anything I've ever shared with just a friend.

"Hi Rafa," he says, beaming brightly as the moon.

"Hello, Ash," I say, outshining the stars.

He surveys my face, which is plastered with uncontainable elation, and I watch as his eyes drift down my body to my bare legs. Opting not to put on sweatpants was definitely the right choice.

"I'm sorry I disappeared on you the other night. I know I keep doing that."

"Yeah, you kind of do," I say, not demanding an explanation but hoping for one all the same.

"I don't know how to explain it."

A wild idea crosses through my head and it pours out of my mouth before I can stop it.

"You don't have a girlfriend or something, do you?"

I visualize a tall, beautiful pre-med student, and my stomach twists unpleasantly.

"What?" He fumbles, "no. It's nothing like that."

"Good," I blurt. Again, before I can stop myself.

"So... you'd be upset if I had a girlfriend?" he asks, raising an eyebrow.

"Not if she made you happy."

His eyebrow returns to its resting place, and I detect a hint of disappointment.

"But yeah, maybe a little," I confess.

A wry curl tugs at the corners of his lips as he reaches for my hand, and I don't pull away. Electricity courses through my every synapse as his fingers weave effortlessly through mine, two vibrant threads that have been longing to be intertwined. I've never held hands with someone before but even so, I'm not nervous.

"I want to show you something," he says, seeking my approval. I nod.
"Show me anything."

We take off into the night. I know I'm not supposed to be running, but a pleasant wind is whipping through my wavy hair and I feel like I'm floating through the trees, levitating above the ground. We disappear into the forest and the scenery zips by, faster and faster until we're practically flying. We're heading in the direction of where I assume he lives, the same direction he came from when he found me that day in the woods. We come to a clearing in the evergreens where the silvery light from the night sky illuminates the sleeping greenery, and the only sounds are bats flitting through the sky and our breath, hot and steady against the cold, silent air.

We stop and stand, our fingers still woven through one another's like wool through a loom. I'm perspiring after darting through the trees, so I let my silk robe fall to the ground and the moonlight soaks into my exposed shoulders. Ash turns to me again, his cobalt eyes absorbing and reflecting the entire Milky Way. He slowly reaches up and touches my cheek so delicately that I tremble with anticipation. I'm not quite sure what's happening, but my body seems to be. My hips turn toward him and I take a step closer, leaving barely a foot between us. He takes a step and closes the gap even more. Ash is so close now that I can smell his breath—sweet peppermint. I feel a hunger growing in my belly, one I've never felt before. It's a hunger for more of him.

"Rafa."

I think he's going to kiss me. I want him to kiss me, like I've never wanted anything before. But, unlike when he took my hand, I'm nervous, and I reach up to scratch my head absentmindedly. When I touch my forehead, I am shocked to find soft, smooth skin– as fresh and new as a baby's.

"My stitches... They're–gone."

Ash nods his head; I'm telling him something he already knows. He pulls away and studies me, as if deciding whether or not to trust me. I touch his hand to tell him that he can, and he squeezes it, believing me.

His hands travel to the base of his shirt and he lifts it up, slowly, purposefully, exposing his torso. I have such a strong urge to touch him that I have to cement my arms to my sides to keep from acting on it. He points to the smooth, flawless skin of his stomach.

"There's a bruise here," he says. The place he points to is devoid of injury, but I remember the wound from the day of the rainstorm. I wonder if he knows I saw. I get the feeling he does.

"Or at least, there's supposed to be," he continues, "but sometimes it's just, gone. Like suddenly everything is healed, and nothing hurts."

115

I touch the pink skin of my forehead. Ash meets my fingertips and traces his thumb down the silhouette of my face, pausing where the stitches should be.

"Your arm," he asks. "Does it hurt?"

I bend my splinted arm gingerly to test it, and it follows my movements easily. I rip off the splint and roll my wrist around, feeling no pain.

"I don't understand."

"Neither do I." He says. "It's like...when I'm with you, my bruise is healed"

"And my accident never happened."

I touch his skin and get that feeling you have right before you wake up on Sunday morning, when you're only half-conscious and all the pains and problems of Monday are a day away, yet you know you don't have much time. His skin is foreign to my touch, otherworldly, yet I feel like I'm sinking into the comfort of something I've always known.

"What are you thinking?" He asks.

"Sometimes I wonder if–if this is a dream."

"Well then I'm dreaming all the time."

"And I want to be," I say. He takes my hand.

"Rafa?"

I cling to each syllable, wishing he would say my whole name just so I can hear his voice for a little while longer. Ash looks like he's about to say more but appears to lose his train of thought before he can verbalize it. He opens his mouth again to speak, but nothing comes out. He reaches for his throat and looks at me, fear invading his eyes.

"What is it?" I ask.

His hands fumble at his windpipe and he starts gagging desperately, grotesquely for air.

"What is it? Are you having a reaction to something? Choking?" But there's nothing to choke on, and no symptoms of an allergy. He's just drowning in the dark air that surrounds us.

"Ash!" I throw my arms around his torso which, just minutes ago was smooth as porcelain. I attempt to give him the Heimlich Maneuver, though I hardly know the form. I place my fist under his ribcage as he sputters and gags, and when I bring my other arm around and squeeze, he buckles forward in pain and I see a flash of swollen, black and blue skin above his waistline and my sprained arm starts to burn again, worse than ever before.

Ash is down on the ground, frantically trying to get air. I kneel down beside him, begging him to breathe. I touch his arm to comfort him, and it's unnaturally cold, as though I'm touching a corpse. As I'm fruitlessly trying to help him, a sharp pain ricochets through my head, bouncing from the base of my skull to my forehead. I reach up to hold my own head and discover a hot, wet trickle–my own blood. I bring my hand down to study the blood and find a loose staple, and a steady stream of thick, red liquid trickling down my cheek.

He looks at me in horror, still clutching his throat. Then, for no reason I can explain, a sudden wave of calm washes over him and he's okay. Ash touches my cheek again, then pulls me in and kisses my forehead. His lips are icy but they soothe the white hot wound on my temple, like aloe to a sunburn. Electric sparks permeate from where his lips meet my skin. I close my eyes and soak up as much of him as I can, as much as I'm allowed. I angle my chin up toward him, wanting more, my body taking over once again. But I feel him slipping away, as if he's fading into the background, dissolving like watercolors while I remain acrylic. Then, just as our lips are about to meet, the sparks disappear, and so does he.

RAFA AND THE REAL BOY IS AVAILABLE ON AMAZON.COM
AND WHEREVER BOOKS ARE SOLD ONLINE.

Made in the USA
Middletown, DE
14 October 2021